Write a
Brilliant CV

Sara Miller McCune founded SAGE Publishing in 1965 to support the dissemination of usable knowledge and educate a global community. SAGE publishes more than 1000 journals and over 800 new books each year, spanning a wide range of subject areas. Our growing selection of library products includes archives, data, case studies and video. SAGE remains majority owned by our founder and after her lifetime will become owned by a charitable trust that secures the company's continued independence.

Los Angeles | London | New Delhi | Singapore | Washington DC | Melbourne

SUPER
QUICK
SKILLS

Write a Brilliant CV

Lucinda Becker

Los Angeles | London | New Delhi
Singapore | Washington DC | Melbourne

Los Angeles | London | New Delhi
Singapore | Washington DC | Melbourne

SAGE Publications Ltd
1 Oliver's Yard
55 City Road
London EC1Y 1SP

SAGE Publications Inc.
2455 Teller Road
Thousand Oaks, California 91320

SAGE Publications India Pvt Ltd
B 1/I 1 Mohan Cooperative Industrial Area
Mathura Road
New Delhi 110 044

SAGE Publications Asia-Pacific Pte Ltd
3 Church Street
#10-04 Samsung Hub
Singapore 049483

Editor: Jai Seaman
Editorial assistant: Lauren Jacobs
Production editor: Victoria Nicholas
Marketing manager: Catherine Slinn
Cover design: Shaun Mercier
Typeset by: C&M Digitals (P) Ltd, Chennai, India

Library of Congress Control Number: 2019954117

British Library Cataloguing in Publication data

A catalogue record for this book is available
from the British Library

ISBN 978-1-5297-1522-4

Contents

Everything in this book! 4

Section 1   What does a CV do?..................................... 7

Section 2   What myths can I ignore? 19

Section 3   What is a 'central CV'? 31

Section 4   What are my professional attributes? 51

Section 5   Why and how should I target my CV? 61

Section 6   How do I introduce myself on my CV? 71

Section 7   How do I show how valuable I am?.......... 81

Section 8   What will make my education and
             training look impressive? 91

Section 9   How will my career history help me?...... 101

Section 10   What should my additional information
             include? 113

Section 11   It is complete – what do I do now?......... 123

Final checklist: How to know you are done 132

Glossary 134

Further resources 136

Everything in this book!

Section 1   What does a CV do?

You can only write a brilliant CV if you know what you are trying to do with it, so let's get this straight right at the beginning.

Section 2   What myths can I ignore?

There are plenty of 'rules' about CVs that just hold you back. You are in control, so you need to know what you do *not* need to do – let's bust some myths.

Section 3   What is a 'central CV'?

Your CV works best if it is targeted at an organization and role, and if it focuses perfectly on exactly what a potential employer needs. A central CV is your starting point.

Section 4   What are my professional attributes?

Graduate attributes, personal qualities, unique selling points – they all come down to the same thing: what makes you good at what you do?

Section 5   Why and how should I target my CV?

A generic CV will not show you in your best light and, worse still, a potential employer might be offended that you did not make the effort.

Section 6   How do I introduce myself on my CV?

Getting started on writing a CV is daunting, and you must make a good first impression: this section shows you how.

Section 7   How do I show how valuable I am?

Just saying you are a great fit for a role is not nearly as persuasive as proving that you are a great fit, and that starts here.

Section 8   What will make my education and training look impressive?

You need not be tied down by every course you have ever taken. Now is the time to step back and be selective.

Section 9   How will my career history help me?

In this section, we will assess and frame your career history to make it easy for an employer to choose you.

Section 10   What should my additional information include?

Nothing boring. Nothing irrelevant. Nothing confusing. Nothing at all that does not urge the employer to see what an asset you will be.

Section 11   It is complete – what do I do now?

Put your CV on your fridge door and admire it. Really, you must do that first! Then work through this section to make the most of it.

What does a CV do?

10 second summary

You can only write a brilliant CV if you know what you are trying to do with it, so let's get this straight right at the beginning.

60 second summary

Know what you are trying to achieve

A CV is designed to do one main job: to give you the chance to go to an interview and shine in front of an employer. It does not replace an application form (which you might also be asked to write) and it does not need to include any information that you feel uncomfortable about providing. It is your chance to be in complete control of the face you present to the world.

How your CV can work for you

Before we begin to work together on your CV, it is important to recognize three super important things about any CV:

1. Its main purpose is to get you through the door of an interview, nothing more than that. It can be the one and only chance you get to make a brilliant first impression and get to that interview.

2. It will help you develop a sense of your professional self: your CV is who you are and shows who you could be.

3. If it does not boost your confidence, you need to review it: your CV should always make you feel at your best.

With these thoughts in mind, this guide will take you through every stage of writing your CV, with practical, effective steps you can take to make it brilliant. There will be exercises to take, tips to bear in mind and plenty of guidance to every aspect of your CV. Making your CV brilliant takes some hard work, but it is never a waste of time: it will all be worth it when you succeed and start your great new job.

A student told us

'I thought a CV was just another type of official form, once I knew how much control I had, it started to feel much more like my CV.'

Learning to reflect

Much of the work of producing a brilliant CV has nothing to do with writing: it requires reflection and some honest, sharp thinking about who you are and where you want to be. That is why the first three sections of this book help you reach the point where you can write an effective CV. It is quicker to think, reflect, and then write than to throw yourself into producing a draft CV that you then change time and time again, never quite sure whether you are making it better or worse.

Reflection can be helped by talking, but with your CV there is a danger to this. You run the risk of your family and friends trying to help you create a CV that reflects how they see you, rather than how you would want an employer to see you. A more objective judge, such as a tutor or careers advisor, might assume that you are simply going to present the strengths you have as a student, which is not going to help you move ahead if you want to change direction or leave some of your student life behind you.

So, your supporters can help you best if you decide in advance who can help and in what way. You will need advisors who know where you want your career to be (even vaguely), you need supporters who will be honest with you, and you need some fresh eyes every now and then.

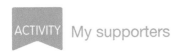

My supporters

Completing this exercise now will help you get these people in place early.

In the first column, note down why you are asking that person for help (they have known you a long time, they are a previous co-worker or manager, they know the job market in your area, they are a careers advisor or professional mentor, a fellow student who knows about your ambitions, a university or college tutor ...).

In the second column, make sure to include that person's full name and contact details (in case you need to use this supporter as a referee later).

The final column will help you ask the right people for help at the right time; a careers advisor might see an early draft, whereas you might only share your CV with a professional mentor at the final stages, so in this column you will note down 'early', 'midway', 'final draft', or 'repeatedly'.

Referee The person who is prepared, having looked at all the documentation, to write a reference that attests to your suitability for a position. This is a targeted document, reflecting both your CV and the role for which you are applying (a general piece of written praise for you is called a 'testimonial'). It is worth noting that your reference might be provided by the HR department of a previous employer, simply confirming the dates you were employed.

Jot down your thoughts below!

Why?	Who?	When?

Choosing your layout

A CV is quite a simple document. It would usually be made up of these sections, often in this order:

Your details: name, contact information, a personal profile.

The key skills you have to offer: as long as you know exactly what skills are needed. If you do not know, then you are not ready to write your CV for that vacancy.

Your education and training: but only in this prime location if your recent education and training link well to the vacancy. If not, you might push this further down the CV.

Your career history: this might be in the form of a chronological account of your career to date (most recent first) or it might be a list of types of work you have carried out (a functional list – more on this later, in the career history section of this guide).

Additional information: this is a great place to give your case a final push, so it must always be both reassuring and impressive.

This layout can alter to suit your 'professional self' and the organization you are targeting, but if you do not have any reason to change the layout, the version given above would be your best option. Your CV would not, without very good reason, exceed two pages of A4: longer, and you risk looking self-important or unable to be succinct; shorter, and you might appear ill-equipped to do the job.

'Your CV is the friend who gets you into the room: after that, you can do the talking.'

CHECK LIST — Test yourself!

☐ Do you know the three main purposes of a CV?

☐ Do you have a list of supporters?

☐ Are you clear about how each supporter can help?

☐ Is the layout of a typical CV clear in your mind?

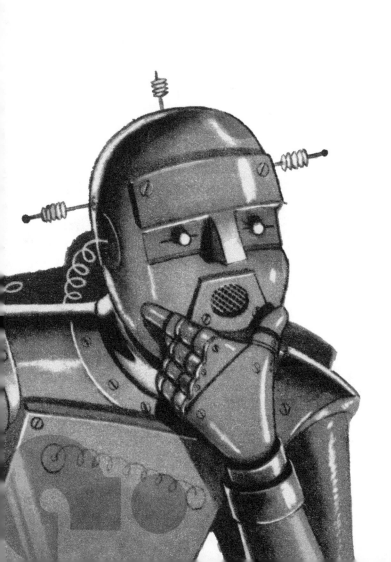

What myths can
I ignore?

*10 second
summary*

There are plenty of 'rules' about CVs
that just hold you back. You are in
control, so you need to know what you
do *not* need to do – let's bust some
myths.

Busting the myths of CVs

There are myths around CVs because writing a CV makes people anxious.
You do not need to be anxious at all because we are working on your CV
together. We need to get all the false rules you think you might have heard
out of the way. Your only focus needs to be on you, and what makes you
an attractive asset to your target organizations.

Myth-busting quiz

Now that you have thought about the overall purpose of your CV, and decided who can help you most, you need to rid yourself of the myths. This quiz will help.

Circle 'true' or 'false' or 'perhaps' to each statement, then look at the answer section that follows to see how many myths you managed to bust!

1 **My CV must contain my full name and current address.**
True / False / Perhaps

2 **A CV written in a coloured font helps to make it stand out.**
True / False / Perhaps

3 **A photo of myself will help make my case to employers.**
True / False / Perhaps

4 **I must include phone, email and social media contact points.**
True / False / Perhaps

5 **I will have one, perfect CV by the end of this book.**
True / False / Perhaps

6 **My National Insurance (NI) number must be included at the end of my CV.**
True / False / Perhaps

7 **Bullet points in a CV can put off potential employers.**
True / False / Perhaps

8 **Only paid work is included in the career history section.**
True / False / Perhaps

9   **My CV will work best if it covers two sides of A4.**
    True / False / Perhaps

10 **Letting a job agency style my CV will boost my chances.**
    True / False / Perhaps

11 **Each job I have done should be listed chronologically.**
    True / False / Perhaps

12 **My hobbies should show ambition and adventure.**
    True / False / Perhaps

13 **I must include my gender on my CV.**
    True / False / Perhaps

14 **I should attach testimonials to my CV.**
    True / False / Perhaps

15 **If there are gaps in my CV, an employer will not want me.**
    True / False / Perhaps

16 **The font I use on my CV is irrelevant.**
    True / False / Perhaps

17 **My referees' names and addresses must be on my CV.**
    True / False / Perhaps

18 **My date of birth must be on my CV.**
    True / False / Perhaps

19 **My referees must be managers or academic tutors.**
    True / False / Perhaps

20 **I should put every qualification I have on my CV.**
    True / False / Perhaps

Answers (maybe...)

Tip!

> The 'maybe' in brackets above is because every single aspect of your CV depends on the career you are targeting, the unique situation you are in, and the experience you have lived so far. I can give you good advice here, but if you know you have reason to do something differently, you will decide, with your supporters, which choice to make.
>
> It is also for this reason that the answers here are fuller than just true, false, or perhaps.

1   **My CV must contain my full name and current address.**

False – you need to include the name you would like to hear when you first enter the room for interview. If you have not used your full, formal name for years, your more usual, familiar name might be better (unless you think it gives the wrong impression of the person you plan to become, or it would make you feel too casual at the start of an interview). There is no point in putting your current address if you are about to graduate: put the address where someone can find you (and this might just be an email address).

2   **A CV written in a coloured font helps to make it stand out.**

Perhaps – it will stand out, but maybe for the wrong reasons: green ink can be very off-putting if you are looking for a good team player to fit into your traditional, reliable firm.

3   **A photo of myself will help make my case to employers.**

False – a photo of yourself reveals your gender, which might put you out of the running altogether in a gender-neutral selection process. Employers will also make assumptions based on what they see, not on what you are proving to them in your CV. The only exception to this might be if you are entering a career area that is a million miles from your qualifications but you think (and have been told) that your face would fit brilliantly. For example, if you are clearly an outdoor, windswept, fit person who wants to be a surf instructor despite having a degree in accountancy and living miles from the sea.

4   **I must include phone, email, and social media contact points.**

False – an interviewer needs to be able to get hold of you, so you need only offer the most accessible (and regularly checked) contact point.

5   **I will have one, perfect CV by the end of this book.**

False – completely false! You will have a 'central CV', which can be used to produce a targeted CV for every career opportunity you find.

> **Central CV** A catalogue of all your skills, personal qualities, attributes, qualifications, experience, employment, professional activities, achievements, and additional information; you will create each targeted CV from a selection of this material.

6   **My NI number must be included at the end of my CV.**

False – although your NI number may be required on an application form, this is not the case for a CV.

7   **Bullet points in a CV can put off potential employers.**

Perhaps – a CV that is too succinct is difficult to read, but bullet points help us to navigate a document, so they should not be avoided.

8 **Only paid work is included in the career history section.**

False – any work you have done (an unpaid internship, voluntary or charity work, professional work as part of your hobbies, and so forth) that has helped you develop professionally should be included.

9 **My CV will work best if it covers two sides of A4.**

True – any longer, and you risk looking self-important or unable to be succinct; shorter, and you might appear ill-equipped to do the job.

10 **Letting a job agency style my CV will boost my chances.**

False – letting *anyone else* take control of your CV could ruin your chances.

11 **Each job I have done should be listed chronologically.**

Perhaps – if your experience shows that you are the right fit for the job; if not, you might consider the functional CV that we will explore together in Section 7 of this guide.

> Functional CV A CV that relies on its career history section by highlighting the professional functions you have performed rather than just listing your job roles.

12 **My hobbies should show ambition and adventure.**

Perhaps – if you are entering a career that requires you to be ambitious and adventurous and you can talk about your hobbies enthusiastically.

13 **I must include my gender on my CV.**

False – there is no requirement to do this. This might actually put you out of the running in a gender-neutral selection process.

14   **I should attach testimonials to my CV.**

False – unless you are specifically asked to do so. Make it easy for the potential employer to invite you to an interview with only as much focused material as you need to get there.

15   **If there are gaps in my CV, an employer will not want me.**

Perhaps – if you have done absolutely nothing for a year, and make this clear on your CV, you might make an interviewer anxious, but this will not be the case for you, because your CV will reflect the person you are and the benefits you bring to an employer, rather than where you were every moment of your life.

16   **The font I use on my CV is irrelevant.**

Perhaps – but this is rarely the case. Times New Roman is usually the font used for studying: universities and colleges still routinely use it. Make it simple for your potential employer to recognize you as 'one of us' by using a professional font such as Arial or Calibri.

17   **My referee's names and addresses must be on my CV.**

False – simply saying 'References available on request' would give you more space to include material that is more persuasive than your referees' names and addresses. As with so much about CVs, this will rely on your research; in some professions, full details of referees on your CV will be expected.

18   **My date of birth must be on my CV.**

False – you need not be judged by your age unless you think it is to your benefit.

19   **My referees must be managers or academic tutors.**

Perhaps – unlike an application form, a CV does not require any
particular type of referee, but it usually makes sense to have at
least one professional contact available.

20   **I should put every qualification I have on my CV.**

False – some of your qualifications may be disappointing, or
irrelevant. As we work through this book together, you will develop
a better sense of the 'you' that is being presented in your CV, and
you will be clearer about whether or not you choose to include
every qualification you have on your CV.

'Take charge and make it work
for you – an idle CV is a
pointless CV.'

CHECK LIST How did you do?

☐ If you already have a CV, do you know what to drop from it now?

☐ Are you happy with what you should be including in your CV?

☐ Do you feel more in control of your CV now?

What is a
'central CV'?

10 second
summary

Your CV works best if it is targeted
at an organization and a role, and if
it focuses perfectly on exactly what
a potential employer needs. A central
CV is your starting point.

60 second
summary

Making the most of everything you have achieved

We all believe that we have areas for improvement and sometimes this can feel overwhelming, but in fact you have far more to offer an employer than you realize. By creating a CV that contains all the great things you can say about yourself – and that ditches anything you are really not interested in doing – you will feel more confident. You will also have a brilliant collection of material ready to go for your targeted CV.

How a central CV works

Removing the myths gives us the freedom to begin on your CV with confidence, but you will not be producing just one CV – you will need several. Every position you go for is different; even if two vacancies ask for identical skills and experience, employers are still likely to prioritize them differently, and it is vital that you notice this.

Tip!

> Simply offering an identical CV to every employer will guarantee that you miss the chance to show each employer that you care about that particular organization and that specific job. Even changing the order of your list of skills will resonate with an employer.

A central CV is a document that is likely to become much longer than the two pages you are aiming to send out to an employer. It will include *all* the material you might include in a CV, and you will pick from this material each time you produce your CV, deciding on the best material to choose and the most effective order in which to place it.

A student told us

> 'I always felt I had too much to say, and I couldn't see my way clearly through it. Putting it all in a central CV gave me back control.'

How to make a central CV

One of the great benefits of a central CV is that you can add to it at any time. You might reword each section a little, to make it even more tightly focused on the job you want, but essentially much of the hard work is done by the time you need to produce each CV.

When you start to produce your central CV, you will not want to be over-whelmed with detail, so it makes sense to log, as speedily as you can, just the overall points you want to make in each section of your CV.

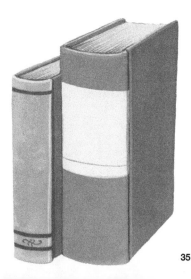

The skeleton of your central CV

There will be five areas to focus on in your central CV: your qualifications, your career history, your skills, your additional information, and any particular achievements that you would like to include somewhere if you get the chance. You could use a separate document for each of these areas or include them in one table. You must not feel any restriction of space (even a table of key notes such as this can run to a surprising number of pages).

You might begin working on your skeleton here, to help get you started as you read this book:

My qualifications	Date, awarding body, grade or classification (throughout this exercise, list everything, even if you are not sure you will use it)

My career experience (including unpaid work) in chronological order with the most recent first: put the job or role here	Dates and organizations for whom I worked

List of my skills	Where have I used or developed that skill?

My additional info (including driving status, language skills, hobbies and interests, first aid training, health and safety awareness, travel experience ...)	More details so that you can keep track of what you have done

My achievements (these might end up in any section of your CV, but it helps to list them separately)	What does this prove about me that would appeal to an employer?

By the end of this exercise, you are still a long way from the CV you might send to an employer, but you have noted down plenty (perhaps most) of the material that you would want to include in your central CV. If you return to this exercise every now and then, you are likely to think of more material to include.

Your next move will be to expand these points to make a persuasive statement from each of them. Take your time over this – small steps are usually better than trying to produce your central CV in one long writing session.

Tip!

You never actually complete your central CV, and you would not want to ... it is a living document that is refined by you throughout your career.

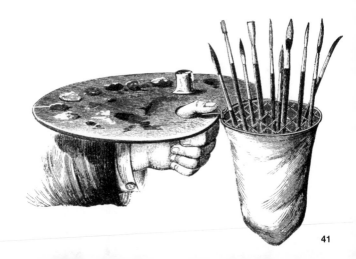

There are three crucial steps that you need to take before you go any further – you need to decide:

1   What (in an ideal world) would you like to leave behind you in your professional journey?

2   What (if you could) would you like to be only a minor part of your future roles?

3   What (because it is important) would make you really love parts of your work life?

By deciding early on what is staying and what might be going, you are in the best possible position to make a good judgement. If you can, you need to dismiss from your mind any career you are already targeting, or feel you should target, and just think of the sort of work you would like to do if you were given a completely free choice. The exercise here focuses on your skills, but it works well with other features of your CV as well.

Complete the following task to make sure you effectively prioritize your skills:

1 Take nine postcard-sized pieces of paper or card (sticky notes will do).
2 Write one skill that you have on each of the cards.
3 Arrange them in a diamond pattern, using the priorities on the opposite page.

Once you have your 'diamond nine', you are ready to start making good choices about what skills to highlight on your CV, because this exercise requires you to focus simultaneously on what makes you happy and what will appeal to your target area of the career market. It also includes just nine key skills. This is enough for most CVs, but you could produce several diamonds if you want to divide your keys skills into different aspects of an overall skill (for example, being good at time management could be divided into organization, time keeping, record keeping, prioritizing, and so forth).

Skill that you absolutely want to use as much as possible in your job

Skill that you very much like using and that would be a satisfying part of your job

Skill that is highly developed, that you enjoy, and that you know will help you land a job

Skill that you would be happy to use every day and that you know will be in demand

Skill that you would be happy to use every day and that you know will be in demand

Skill that you would be happy to use every day and that you know will be in demand

Skill that you need to develop but you are unsure as to whether you enjoy using it or not

Skill that you will use if required, but hopefully not too often

Skill that, even if you are very good at it, you really do not want to use in your future career

Make it active: Expanding the range of your diamond nine

This exercise need not be restricted to making choices about your skills. It is also very effective in helping you decide on which type of job to target. You could identify nine aspects of a working life and prioritize them through a diamond nine. I have listed here nine features that are commonly used for this version of the exercise:

1 Money

2 Working hours

3 Distance to work

4 Size of organization

5 Chance to train

6 Leadership opportunities

7 Ethics of the organization

8 Status

9 Size of team

Tip!

This exercise is not easy to do alone, but it is important that you at least have a go at it by yourself to start out, so that your judgement is not clouded by your supporters' opinions.

Once you have a diamond nine (or several) in place, it is important to share. You could do this in two ways: if you carry out the exercise with a group of your fellow students, with each of you producing your own diamond, the way they explain their decision-making will help you as you decide. If you are using one (or more) of your other supporters, you will be revealing to them not necessarily the person they think you are, but the person you plan to become. This can be a valuable moment for you both, as it will help that supporter to work with you more effectively in future.

A student told us

'It was much easier for my family to support me once I began to ask for their help with specific parts of my CV. It really helped them see me as a young professional graduate.'

'I know my professional best when I see myself on paper – that is what I am selling.'

CHECK LIST Got it?

☐ Do you have a good sense of what skills you want to promote on your CV?

☐ Do you know which skills you would like to drop for the future?

☐ Are you clearer now on the main features of the type of career you want to target?

The work you have carried out in this section will give you a good idea of what you *might* want to include in your CV: now we will think about what you *need* to include in the CV that you actually send for each opportunity you find.

What are my professional attributes?

10 second summary

Graduate attributes, personal qualities, unique selling points – they all come down to the same things: what makes you good at what you do?

60 second
summary

Drop the negative

The best way to demonstrate what an asset you could be is to avoid getting too hung up on anything that you feel is negative. Instead, focus on those aspects of your life and personality that make you a catch for an employer. That means working out why you are good at some professional tasks. Once you know why you excel, you can demonstrate that you will always excel in that area.

What are professional attributes?

You may have heard of the phrase 'professional attributes' or 'graduate attributes' and wondered what it means. Attributes are your skills and qualifications, but they are also more than this: they are those things about you that add value to your professional profile. Often, these are personal qualities that you have developed to a high degree.

Some examples of attributes will make this clearer:

Attributes The personal qualities, skills, and level of understanding that would be expected of a graduate. Definitions of graduate attributes vary a little from source to source, and you might also think in terms of professional attributes. These are the qualities, knowledge, and aptitudes expected of a professional in your field.

1   If you are highly skilled in handling complex sets of data, this might be because you are *patient*, or perhaps you have the *stamina* to work for long stretches of time; maybe you have the *vision* to see the bigger picture, or it could be the reverse: you might like to *focus* in great detail.

2   If you are good at presenting, that might be down to your *confidence* or because you *work hard* to prepare, or because you are an adept *communicator*; it might be that you *enjoy the challenge* of the event.

3   If you are a skilled leader in a group, it might not be because you are *forthright* in sharing your views; many leaders succeed because they are *quiet listeners* who can nurture their team, and for some it is because they are neither of these things, but they have developed *orderly minds* and can chair a meeting and keep it to time.

As you will see from these three examples, the skills are clear (data manipulation, presentation skills, and leadership) but the *attributes* that underpin these skills (in italics) can be varied and even contradictory. This is good for you. You never need assume, for example, that you cannot lead a professional group because you are not loud and confident: you can.

It is also great for your CV: rather than just listing your skills, you can share with your potential employer an insight into why you are so accomplished in certain areas. This not only helps to prove that you really have the skill you are claiming, it also reveals attributes that the employer will recognize as valuable in other aspects of the role for which you are applying – everyone wins.

Take your time

Graduate attributes take time to recognize, so there is no need to push yourself too hard in the early stages of producing a CV. Work from your skills (what makes me good at this skill?) and then, every now and again, take a step back and think about whether you have any other attributes that you are not directly revealing through your skills, but which you think might be appealing on your CV. You will see later (in Section 6) that there is space on your CV to share your attributes with an interviewer, regardless of whether or not they are linked to a skill area.

A student told us

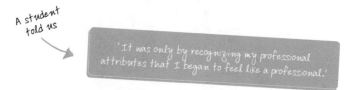

'It was only by recognizing my professional attributes that I began to feel like a professional.'

I mention 'interviewer' here because the idea of attributes takes us a little further than the door of the interview room. The main function of a CV is to get you to that interview, but once you mention attributes and achievements on your CV, you are also sowing the seed for parts of the conversation once you are in the room. Of course, this can only be to your benefit.

'Never undersell yourself in the career market: you will have years to regret it.'

Congratulations

Well done on your hard work so far. We have done vital preparation work. This will not have been easy: it is challenging to work through these exercises, bringing together so much information about yourself and having to consider what makes you an appealing candidate.

Check your understanding

☐ Can you identify your three key skills?

☐ Do you know what makes you so good in those areas?

☐ Can you list your three key personal qualities?

Why and how should
I target my CV?

*10 second
summary*

A generic CV will not show you in your
best light and, worse still, a potential
employer might be offended that you
did not make the effort.

60 second summary

Focus, focus, focus!

Focusing your CV, so that what you are writing about yourself matches up easily and obviously with what an employer wants, is one of the most powerful tools at your disposal. You want an employer to find no reason to doubt your fit, and plenty of reasons to invite you to interview: that is what targeting will do for you.

Targeting your CV

A CV with no focus is a CV that is likely to fail. As soon as a potential employer realizes that you have not bothered to customize your CV for a role, it is obvious you do not care enough about landing the role to make an effort ... your CV is now in the bin. If there are many applicants for a job, any employer will be glad to reduce the pile of CVs on the desk, and this is one of the first excuses anyone would have to discard your CV, so you have to target.

Tip!

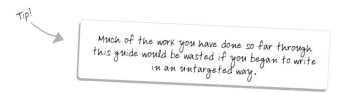

Much of the work you have done so far through this guide would be wasted if you began to write in an untargeted way.

Targeting your CV, that is, making sure that your potential employers and interviewers know that you have created a CV just for their vacancy, brings with it five huge benefits:

- It demonstrates how much you care about the opportunity (who could resist?).

- It proves that you have done your research and know that the vacancy is the right one for you (how reassuring for them).

- It allows you to shine, by showing them exactly how well you would fit into their team, and how many benefits you can offer the organization (how easy it will be for them to choose you for interview).

- It helps to shape the interview (because you have cleverly included some targeted points as topics of conversation).

- It gives you the chance to reflect – if you struggle to target your CV, you might be applying for the wrong job (and you will save yourself time and effort if you just move on to the next opportunity).

Your central CV is your starting point

Most of the work you will carry out to target your CV takes place before you even think of applying for a vacancy. Your central CV is your starting point, so producing this first (even if it is not in its fullest version yet) will allow you to target later by just pulling in the best material for each vacancy.

A student told us

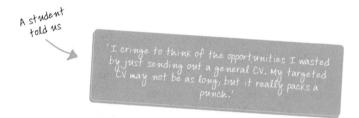

'I cringe to think of the opportunities I wasted by just sending out a general CV. My targeted CV may not be as long, but it really packs a punch.'

In order to target your CV, you need to know as much as you can about a vacancy, so that you can foreground just the skills, experience, and attributes that most appeal to the potential employer. How you do this will depend on how you hear about the opportunity, so here are some ideas about how you might begin your detective work on a vacancy.

Tip!

These lists are not exhaustive, and you will not necessarily use just one of these lists for a vacancy. Remember: the more you know (however you get to know it) the better your chance to target your CV.

Targeting advertised jobs

If a job is advertised:

- Take a highlighter pen to identify each skill and attribute that is mentioned. If the advert is lengthy, you might use different colours to identify what you see as the 'necessary' skills and what you see as simply 'desirable'.

- If a 'job description' or 'person specification' is available, make sure you get a copy and use your highlighter on these, too.

- If there is an email address for further enquiries, or a person you can contact for an 'informal chat' about the job, use it as an opportunity to get ahead of the game, but ignore the word 'informal'. Prepare well, have just a couple of important questions to ask, with material ready if you are asked to talk about yourself in the phone call or email exchange.

- If you contact an organization and it goes well, which it will if you prepare, your name will be remembered. Always note the name of the person you speak to – you want to be able to recognize that person in the interview introductions.

Job description An outline of the duties and responsibilities involved in a role, also including practicalities such as hours of work and salary. It might also indicate the skills and experience needed in an ideal candidate. A brief job description might be in an advertisement or it might be a separate document.

Person specification A description of the ideal person for a role, listing 'necessary/required' experience, qualifications, and attributes as well as those that are 'desirable'.

Targeting jobs you have heard about

If you hear about a vacancy that is not yet being advertised:

- Ask your supporter to give you as much information as possible: especially a contact name.

- Find out if the organization has advertised a similar post recently and check the advert for that post.

- Browse the company website to get a sense of the type of employee that might work there.

- Once you feel confident that you know enough, make contact by phone or email with some well-prepared questions. If you make contact by email, it makes sense to ask first whether you are contacting the best person to answer queries, and to make sure they are happy to chat by email.

Targeting an organization

If you want to approach an organization directly, even though you are not sure if there are any vacancies:

- Decide in advance who to ask for when you call. This might be a contact you already have, a division lead, a name you have noticed on a website or the Human Resources Department, but a receptionist can also be helpful. You may need to go no further on the first call, so do not dismiss that first potential point of contact.

- Prepare a list of things to say about yourself so that you won't become flustered.

- Do not begin by asking about a job; instead, tell them that you admire the organization and would like to work for it, so you would like to know where it advertises vacancies. This might be enough.

- If you are offered more information, such as a specialist website to go to for vacancies, or the details of a further contact, take some time to investigate before you make the next approach. Thoroughness is key to success in this type of searching.

'A CV is like an arrow. It must land squarely in the right place.'

Congratulations

You have now defined your 'professional self' and you know, in a good amount of detail, what your target organization wants from the successful applicant. Finally, you are ready to write!

How do I introduce myself on my CV?

10 second summary

Getting started on writing a CV is daunting, and you must make a good first impression: this section shows you how.

60 second
summary

Making each line count

The work you have done so far puts you in a great position to give the best possible first impression. Most employers read CVs from start to finish, rather than just dipping in, so you need to make sure that every single line counts, and that starts at the very beginning.

Making your first, first impression

The first aspect of introducing yourself has nothing to do with the words you use: it relies on the font you choose. As I mentioned before, your CV is best produced in a font such as Calibri or Arial. I also noted earlier that there are three pieces of information that you do not have to include in the first section of your CV unless you are asked specially or you think they will help you: your date of birth, the full name on your birth certificate and your NI or Identification Number.

Every line of your CV has to help make your case, so you must use the space wisely. So, for example, you might want to write 'Curriculum Vitae' at the head of the document, because that is what it is (CV being the shortened form), but you might decide that it is obviously a CV, you are already tight on space, and because you are the only person applying it shouldn't get lost in a pile of paperwork so you will leave 'Curriculum Vitae' off the document. I have given you this example in detail because you will find some advisors telling you that you have to do something or that you absolutely must not do something. In fact, where you think there is a choice to be made, you will make the best choice for your circumstances.

Tip!

If anyone else (a supporter, your Careers Advisor, an employment agency) tries to help you by taking this choice away from you, make sure that you get the final say on your CV.

What to include at the beginning of your CV

So, what are you likely to include in this opening section of your CV?

Your name: with the first one being the one by which you like to be called, as long as it is not such a casual pet name that interviewers might be put off when they interview you.

Your contact details: an email address (if yours is funny or strident, you might want to create a more professional email address just for your career plans) and a phone number (a number that you know you can usually answer relatively quickly and undisturbed). A postal address can be reassuring, but only along one line – do not waste space. Make sure it is an address that will be current for the entire duration of your career search.

A student told us

'I am so glad I bothered to look properly at the first section of my CV – I had no idea it could do so much for me.'

How a personal profile works

A personal profile would be no longer than 2–3 sentences, is often written in the third person (as if you were writing about someone else) and showcases why you should be employed. Here are some examples:

An energetic team player with a passion for travel. A writer with extensive experience in blog travel writing, keen to branch out into print travel media. Motivated when working alone, but also happy as a productive member of a team.

A highly organized and hardworking individual with a flair for motivating a sales team. Over two years' experience in retail and training in Customer Satisfaction have resulted in a goal-setting approach to each new challenge. A reliable and energetic member of a team, ready to move into a management role.

Combining excellent academic results with a thorough grounding in laboratory techniques, I have always been driven to achieve excellence. My recent success in leading an experimental team has allowed me to develop my listening and organizational skills, with the aim of becoming an effective laboratory team leader in future.

What these all have in common is that they are no more than three sentences and they are highly targeted at a specific role. They combine skills, experience, and attributes and they all stress both the advantages of employing the candidate now and the way in which that person might benefit the organization in the future.

If your profile goes beyond two or three sentences, consider moving some of the material to your 'key skills' section. If you cannot think what to include in your profile, despite all of the work you have done so far, ask yourself whether this is really the right opportunity for you.

If your personal profile reflects you (even if it is a really great version of you, on a particularly good day!) and you know that it also reflects what the organization wants, you can move on with confidence and energy.

'A CV exists to shake the hand of an employer before you get the chance.'

CHECK LIST Targeting your personal profile

A profile must be targeted, so ask yourself these questions:

1   What do they want? Can you highlight the skills, personal qualities, and experience they have asked for?

2   What can I offer? From your central CV, what material can you pick out, being as specific as you can?

3   Where might this lead? Would you want to include in your profile a mention of where you might go in the future, making clear the benefit to the organization of this ambition?

How do I show how valuable I am?

10 second summary

Just saying you are a great fit for a role is not nearly as persuasive as proving that you are a great fit, and that starts here.

60 second summary

Your skills add value to you

Throughout your CV, you will need to prove your potential value, both now and in the future, and this began in your profile. In the next section, in which you outline your skills, you need to be crystal clear about that value. You do this by focusing on the benefit you bring to an employer.

Demonstrating the benefit your skills and attributes can bring to an employer is a three-stage process:

Step one   What skills are being asked for in this role?

Step two   Can I prove I have them?

Step three How do I demonstrate the benefit they bring?

Tip!

> If you see a skill included in the vacancy advert or job description that you do not feel you have, look at the detail – is it a major and essential part of the role, and something the organization is not prepared to offer training in? If you are convinced you could be an asset to the organization despite missing one skill, be bold and produce a CV for the role regardless. If, on the other hand, a major skill needed for the role is in the bottom three of your skills diamond nine, be very cautious about going ahead.

Luckily, you will already know which skills are needed, as you have done your detective work. However, if you do no more than claim to have a list of skills, all you are proving is that you are very good at copying across from an advert or job description onto your CV. This will take you some way towards your goal, and may be enough. It proves that you have engaged with the details of the vacancy and understand what is needed.

But, will it take you far enough? Perhaps not, and if you think you need to do more, you move to Step two. Rather than just claiming that you have a skill, you give an example of that skill in action. This will be far more impressive.

Proving your worth

Step two may be enough, especially if your education, training and career history make clear that this opportunity is a linear progression from your previous activity. If your career aim is not an easy straight line from where you have been, or if you really want to strike home the benefits you are bringing with you, you can take Step three. This involves you thinking about a function of the role, finding from your central CV a skill that suits this function, and then using an example to prove how effective this has been in action. Note that both skills and attributes are included in the example on the following page, as you might feel that both are asked for, even if not directly.

The vacancy calls for: Step one – you could just list these	You have: Step two – you could prove you have the skills	What benefit did you bring? Step three – you could show how your skills have benefited others
Sales skills	A year's experience in retail sales	The shop team I led increased sales by 12% in the final quarter of last year
Motivation	A three-week placement undertaken as part of my course	I was the top placement student in my year and my placement provider used my ideas when launching a new website
IT experience	Undertaken courses in Excel, Word and Onenote	Onenote has allowed me to bring together a diverse team in order to manage an academic project
Marketing skills	Worked as part of a team in promoting the Summer Celebration at my university	Tickets sales increased by 7% compared to last year, despite a drop in student numbers at the university
Language skills	Qualified in three languages	Organized a trip to Germany for my study group, using my language skills to negotiate a reduction in costs

A student told us

'I used to read the skills on the job description and just list them on my CV, with no proof at all. No wonder I had to work really hard in an interview to prove that I was a good person for the job!'

Thinking about references

For each targeted CV, you will need to decide how many proven, beneficial skills to include in your introductory section, and those that you do not list there can be included throughout the rest of your CV. You might also now be able to start thinking in a focused way about your referees. Who can prove your value? Who will be able to verify that you have brought these benefits to others? It may be that the name of a referee springs to mind: now is the time to note it down for future use.

'Believe in yourself and others will agree.'

Congratulations

Once you have produced a table of skills, proof, and benefits, you have the core of your sales pitch. Include this table in your central CV, adding to it each time you apply for a job that demands a skill or an attribute that you have not analysed in this way before.

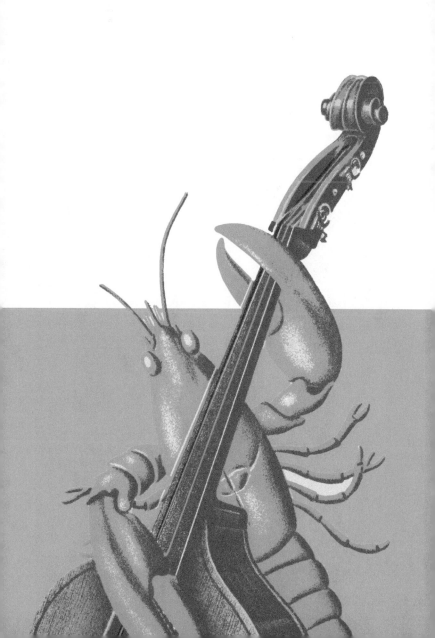

What will make my education and training look impressive?

10 second summary

You need not be tied down by every course you have ever taken. Now is the time to step back and be selective.

60 second
summary

Keeping it positive

You do not want to go into an interview worrying about one training course you failed or one minor qualification you lack. Instead, make best use of the training and qualifications you do have, and remember that it is often cheaper to train someone than to advertise a post because the wrong person for the team was employed first time around. Be brave here: if you are the right person, make it clear and be proud of what you have achieved.

Focus on the reader

In this section of your CV, your focus is on how your education and training will strike the reader. For most of us, for most of our CVs, we would want to include all our qualifications and details of our training successes, so it is a case of deciding how to show what you have done in the best way.

The first thing to note is that you do not have to include every single qualification detail on your CV. If you gained a very low grade in GCSE French, and you are hugely embarrassed by it, simply list your GCSEs without grades. If you once undertook some IT training and failed the course, then leave it off or simply write 'Training received in Excel and Power-Point'. This is not about lying: it is about putting the best version of yourself forward and giving you and your interviewers some good starting points for a conversation.

Education Any course that you undertook at school, college, or university for which you received a nationally recognized qualification (university is sometimes called 'tertiary education'). Education does not usually include training in the workplace.

Training Any instruction and guidance you have received in a formal structure. This might be where you work or in a college or other training base. You may or may not receive a certificate upon completion.

Making best use of your space

You will also need to think about space. You do not have space to place all of your qualifications in lists down the page: pre-university qualifications can be listed in one line, to save space. Your university award will be included, of course, but you do not need to give a classification (1st, 2:1, lower second, and so on) if you would rather not. You also need not list every module or course you took; this gives you space to include some detail of modules that you can talk about persuasively at interview, either because you really enjoyed them and maybe did well in them, or because you know they are directly relevant to the role.

You will notice that I have given examples here of training and educational qualifications. Here is the difference: an educational qualification is one that you have gained from a school, college or university (or similar educational institution) and that is, usually, nationally and internationally recognized. Training is undertaken away from these institutions, is often vocational and may or may not provide you with a certificate. First aid training, for example, will come with certification from a recognized body, but if you took a one-day in-house Customer Satisfaction course as part of your weekend job, even though you did not get a certificate, you would still include this under your training if it is relevant to the role for which you are applying.

Training counts – even if you have not done it all yet

Training that you include on your CV does not have to be completed. If you know that the successful candidate for a vacancy will need to speak some French, for example, you might want to sign up for a course in business French. It can be confidently added to your CV as 'Training being undertaken'. This shows your commitment and willingness to learn new skills.

Highlight your key education and training

Now is a good time to think about how you could bring all this together. There are three tables below, ready for you to list the aspects of your education and training that you want to foreground in your CV and highlight during an interview:

One pre-university qualification or training course that you would like to highlight:
1

Two training courses you think are relevant to the type of vacancy that interests you:
1
2

Three university modules/projects that you are especially proud of:
1
2
3

Once you have produced your education and training section, you need to think about positioning. If what you have learnt and achieved so far leads naturally into the job in which you are interested, it makes sense to place it directly below your list of key skills. If you believe that your career history is a more persuasive tool to gain you an interview, put that above your education and training section. Getting this positioning right will make it easy for a potential employer to see why you are right for a role, and it will keep your confidence high.

Tip!

If you place your education and training section lower on your CV, make sure that you include the word 'graduate' in your profile, so that a potential employer can see at first glance that you are educated to graduate level.

'Your training helped to make you who you are, but it is never the whole story. Be you, and let everything else follow.'

CHECK
LIST

Test yourself!

☐ Are you clear about the differences between education and training?

☐ Are you happy with the qualifications you will include in your CV?

☐ Have you identified every scrap of training you have ever undertaken?

How will my career history help me?

10 second summary

In this section, we will assess and frame your career history to make it easy for an employer to choose you.

Your value is in what you have done, not who paid you

In your CV, you are highlighting your professional value, which means that everything you have done that has involved professional activity has the potential to add to this value. It will not matter if this was paid or unpaid work, or even if you did not really see it as 'work' at all: if you have experience that proves your fit for a role, this is the place to include it.

Making the right impression

The first question you might be asking yourself is, why I am writing about my 'career history' and not my 'employment' or 'work experience'? It is simple: 'employment' gives quite the wrong impression if you want to demonstrate to an employer that you are looking for a fulfilling career rather than just a short-term job. Even if the vacancy for which you are applying is not a magnificent job, by writing about your career history you are showing that you take your career seriously and that you have experience you are proud of. 'Work experience' runs the risk of a potential employer assuming you have never had any paid work (and even if this is the case, it is not something you need stress on a CV).

Tip!

> Whether or not you have been paid to work or carry out any professional activities is irrelevant as far as your CV is concerned. You have done the work and you have gained the professional experience; if it is relevant, it goes on your CV.

What your career history can achieve

As an overview, your career history needs to work in a similar way to your skills; the main purpose of this section of your CV is to:

- Prove that you are used to working in a professional setting.

- Reassure a potential employer that you have been well regarded professionally.

- Demonstrate the skills and experience you have acquired so far.

- Give some sense of where your career might be heading.

- Show that you are a candidate who can benefit a potential employer.

Your challenge will be to do all of this in a relatively small space. This is where bullet points suddenly become your best friend. You cannot simply assume that a potential employer will understand the role you undertook or know the organizations on your CV. An exercise on this will help you condense all the most appealing aspects of your career history onto your central CV, ready to be pulled through on to each targeted CV.

ACTIVITY Career history

Step one: List everything (really, absolutely everything) that you have ever done that has required you to undertake duties or carry out tasks that are relevant to the professional world.

Step two: Ask a friend, family member or other supporter to check the list. It is likely that you have forgotten a college trip that you organized, or a series of articles you wrote for a student newspaper, or the voluntary work you did one summer, or the work you carry out as part of your family's business (especially if it is carried out at home).

Step three: Expand each item on this list to show what was involved. You need to force yourself to drag out every aspect of each role. For example, serving behind a bar in a pub or club becomes:

- Handling cash.
- Dealing with members of the public.
- Marketing and promoting products.
- Working under pressure.
- Responding to complaints.
- Prioritizing tasks.
- Completing work rota spreadsheets.
- Following instructions.
- Learning about new products and procedures.
- Health and safety awareness.
- Working as part of (and/or leading) a team.
- Shift work experience.

Step four: Add to this list (however long or short it is) one or two achievements that you are proud of, or an example or two of your success. So, for the role of bar worker, this might be:

- Receiving Employee of the Month award.
- Increasing sales of a new product by 16% on your shift.
- Receiving a positive comment sent in by a customer.
- Raising £206 for a local charity through the pub quiz.

To get you started, pick a role you have undertaken (either paid or voluntary) and start to break it down here:

Role:	
Skill 1	
Skill 2	
Skill 3	
Skill 4	
Skill 5	
Skill 6	
Achievement	
Success	

Step five: Before going any further, add all this material to your central CV. You will want to manipulate it in various ways for each targeted CV you produce, so keep it safe in its entirety at this point.

What is a functional CV?

In thinking about how to mould your material to make it most persuasive, you could consider a functional section to your CV. Many CVs will simply give a list of posts that have been held, with a series of bullet points beneath each job title, to show what it involved (a standard chronological CV). However, if you have had eight jobs before you even reached the graduate job market and they were all very much the same or if you had a few significant jobs but also lots of minor professional roles, you might want to group these together to save space and create impact.

> **Chronological CV** A CV that shows your career history in chronological order, one role after the other, with the most recent (or the current) role listed first.

This might take the form of just one entry, such as:

2014–2019: Various office roles undertaken, including sales support, spreadsheet maintenance, travel planning, diary management, and minute taking.

This could cover five different temporary jobs you undertook over three summers and using this approach can highlight just what is relevant to your target role, rather than asking your potential employer to wade through too much text, hunting for what is relevant.

If you are including significant and relevant roles in your career history section, but you have experience from a minor voluntary role or family business that you know would be appealing, you might add an entry such as this:

> Throughout my career, I have undertaken bookkeeping for charities and a family business. I therefore have a high level of attention to detail and good financial awareness.

Again, you are not listing dates, job titles, or organizations, but you are pointing out a breadth of experience that might tip the selection process in your favour.

Use your options

It is possible to produce an entire career section as functional, showing in some detail your areas of professional activity, with just a list of employers and dates above or below. You might want to aim for a mixed CV, which relies mainly on dates, organization, and job title on one line, with a list of duties bullet-pointed below, followed by a couple of achievements or successes, but which also collates several roles together for one or two of your entries.

Tip!

> You can list outcomes alongside duties in this section of your CV. Rather than simply asserting that you led a team, add a positive result of your actions (such as, staff turnover reduced in 2019); rather than just noting that you dealt with members of the public, add that you received a 100% satisfaction score. This is the same as your list of skills – make it easy for a potential employer to see the benefits to be gained by hiring you.

Whatever decisions you make about what to include in your career history section, and how to present this, you will be guided by all the research you have done on the organization and the role. You will highlight most firmly the aspects of your career that most neatly fit with the highest priority duties of the role. The challenge is made simpler by your research: make it easy for you to be the successful candidate.

'You are a great catch because your life made you that way.'

What should my additional information include?

10 second summary

Nothing boring. Nothing irrelevant. Nothing confusing. Nothing at all that does not urge the employer to see what an asset you will be.

Making a brilliant last impression

It is all too easy to think that additional information means 'all the bits of information that do not quite fit anywhere else', but this would be a missed opportunity. Everything in this final section of your CV must serve at least one of two purposes: it must prove that there is no reason why you should not be hired, or it should persuade the reader that you are the best person for the job.

Taking a rounded view of yourself

This is a dangerous section of your CV, because there is a temptation to throw anything into it that does not quite fit anywhere else, or to use it for irrelevant and mundane information that somehow you think you should include. Resist this temptation: this is your chance to make a brilliant last impression on your CV. It is likely to be no more than a third of a page, and may be less, so use every single line to your advantage.

Here is a list of items that you might include:

1   Any of your hobbies and interests that would especially appeal to your potential employer (that is, they show personal qualities or demonstrate skills that will be valued in your target organization).

2   Any skills that you have not included elsewhere (a language you are learning, for example, or a skill that is not relevant to the role but that is unusual or an interesting talking point at interview).

3   Any achievements that you have not included elsewhere (perhaps recognition for voluntary work, a challenge award, or a public event in which you featured).

4   Practical accomplishments that would be valuable (driving licence, first aid, and similar).

5   If you think it would help your case, you might include your date of birth.

6   Any professional affiliation you have, such as student/associate membership of a body that regulates or supports your target professional area.

A student
told us

'My friends and I always used to put the same
three interests on our CV – I'm not sure we were
thinking about the impression we were making. Now
that I have improved it, I know I have talking
points ready for interviews.'

Making your additional information work hard for you

Treat this section as any other in your CV – it needs to make your case and it needs to lead a potential employer to put your CV on the 'interview pile'. It is also the section that interviewers will use to find easy topics of conversation during your interview. Although many of the questions you are asked will be standard and put to all candidates, there is often space left in the interview for more general conversation, and your additional information section will help you to guide that conversation in a direction that favours you.

'On a CV, you have never done anything
"just for fun": everything counts, and
anything might be important.'

CHECK LIST — Ask yourself!

☐ Does your CV end as impressively as it begins?

☐ Would you want to employ you?

☐ Could your additional information lead to interesting interview conversations?

Congratulations

You know how to create a central CV, you have a detective path to follow and you recognize the ways in which you can target your CV to make it brilliant for the role you have chosen. All the hard work is done, and you are ready to make it work for you!

It is complete – what do I do now?

10 second
summary

Put your CV on your fridge door and admire it. Really, you must do that first! Then work through this section to make the most of it.

60 second
summary

Stay in control

Keeping control of your CV is going to be a priority at this stage. Be selective about where you send it, produce a freshly targeted CV for each vacancy (even if there are only slight differences between the adverts or job descriptions) and make sure that the format stays stable. Keeping a record of where your CV has gone (and which version you sent) will take up some time, but it will be worth it. This is your brilliant CV – protect it and make it work hard!

Thinking about referees again

The first question to ask yourself before you complete your CV is whether you want to send it out into the world with referees listed on it. This can be reassuring, giving you the sense that you have guaranteed support: anyone who wants to interview you can receive an endorsement from your referees. On the other hand, you might want to know that an offer is being considered before you send your referees all the documentation so that they can produce a perfectly targeted reference.

You are also unlikely to rely on just two referees; different opportunities might call for the support of different referees. You might also feel that including details of your referees takes up valuable space on your CV that could better be used to make your case. 'References available on request' is a phrase that you might prefer to include, unless you are specifically asked to include details of referees on your CV, or your referees are so well known and esteemed in your field that their names alone would act as an inducement to select you for interview.

A freelancer's CV

It might be that your CV is not intended to gain you a place at interview for a single vacancy. If you are a freelance professional, or running your own business, your CV will be targeted at a slightly wider area of the business marketplace so that it showcases a good range of your skills and experience, ready for different potential clients or customers.

I have already urged you to keep control of your CV, rather than letting any third parties 'style it' for you, but this is not always possible to do: your professional field might rely so heavily on agencies that you have to let it be used by third parties. Despite this, control will still be important, and you will need to agree to any changes.

Keeping track of your CV

Keeping control rests also with keeping good records. For each application, you need to keep a copy of the advert, job description and person specification (if these exist), a log of any contact you made with the organization, and a copy of the targeted CV you used for this opportunity. This might seem laborious, but it ensures that you are never left wondering which version of your CV the interviewers are reading, or meeting someone you suspect you have already talked to at some point, but not being quite sure. It also means that you are not without vital information if the material about the vacancy was on a website and is removed once the closing date for application has passed.

Searching out a series of good career opportunities can take time, so keeping this record of what you have done will help you if an organization contacts you months after you sent in your CV. If things go quiet for a while, your records will keep you motivated, reminding you of how much ground you have covered.

Your CV online and on paper

If you are emailing out your CV, remember to send it as a PDF so that it reaches its destination in perfect format and always send it as an attachment rather than trying to embed it within an email. This can distort its layout and make it difficult to send on to other people in the selection process.

Although you will often be sending your CV by email or lodging it online (perhaps as part of a professional website you have created), a paper copy of your CV is also valuable. If you keep a copy on you whenever you are in a professional setting, you can hand it out to new contacts, or to professionals who could advise you on your career plans. If you call an organization to enquire about possible opportunities, having a paper CV in front of you ensures you are ready to respond to any questions you are asked. It is a good idea to have a printout of your CV on you at interview, but only refer to it if you really need to check on some detail. Generally speaking, you are trying for an interview that is more of a conversation than a test.

Just as importantly as all of this, you can attach your CV to your fridge door and glance at it from time to time: this is simple, but a great way to keep reminding yourself of your impressive professional self.

'No CV ever helped anyone by sitting in a computer: it needs to work for you and it needs to work hard.'

Final checks

☐ When you glance at your CV, does the layout look clean and inviting?

☐ Have you wasted any space on your CV?

☐ Now that it is done, does it make you feel good about yourself?

Congratulations

You are perfectly prepared to present yourself to the professional world, knowing that you are making the best use of every scrap of relevant material and confident that you have a CV that will support you during an interview. Now you can take the next step: from a brilliant CV to a brilliant career!

Final checklist: How to know you are done

Do you have a clear sense of the principal purposes of your CV? ☐

Have you listed your supporters, and do you feel in control of your CV? ☐

Are you producing material for a central CV, ready to target your CV for each opportunity you find? ☐

Is it clear that you have particular skills, experiences, and qualities that make you valuable to an employer? ☐

Have you done enough research to produce powerful and persuasive CVs for your target career area? ☐

If you just glance at your CV, does it look clear and impressive? ☐

Does your profile at the top of your CV genuinely reflect your professional self, as well as being targeted at your potential employer? ❏

Do you have plenty of examples ready to prove your value? ❏

Have your supporters confirmed that you have included all your relevant training and education? ❏

Is it easy to see the relevance of all the material in your career history section? ❏

Does your additional information section increase the impact of your CV? ❏

Your CV should make you feel good about yourself – is it pinned up somewhere so that you can admire it regularly? ❏

Glossary

Attributes   The personal qualities, skills, and level of understanding that would be expected of a graduate. Definitions of graduate attributes vary a little from source to source, and you might also think in terms of professional attributes. These are the qualities, knowledge, and aptitudes expected of a professional in your field.

Central CV   A catalogue of all your skills, personal qualities, attributes, qualifications, experience, employment, professional activities, achievements, and additional information; you will create each targeted CV from a selection of this material.

Chronological CV   A CV that shows your career history in chronological order, one role after the other, with the most recent (or the current) role listed first.

CV personal profile   Two or three sentences that offer a concise overview of your professional self, targeted at a specific role.

Education   Any course that you undertook at school, college or university for which you received a nationally recognized qualification (university is sometimes called 'tertiary education'). Education does not usually include training in the workplace.

Functional CV   A CV that relies on its career history section by highlighting the professional functions you have performed rather than just listing your job roles.

Job description   An outline of the duties and responsibilities involved in a role, also including practicalities such as hours of work and salary. It might also indicate the skills and experience needed in an ideal candidate. A brief job description might be in an advertisement or it might be a separate document.

Person specification   A description of the ideal person for a role, listing 'necessary/required' experience, qualifications and attributes as well as those that are 'desirable'.

Referee   The person who is prepared, having looked at all the documentation, to write a reference that attests to your suitability for a position. This is a targeted document, reflecting both your CV and the role for which you are applying (a general piece of written praise for you is called a 'testimonial'). It is worth noting that your reference might be provided by the HR department of a previous employer, simply confirming the dates you were employed.

Training   Any instruction and guidance you have received in a formal structure. This might be where you work or in a college or other training base. You may or may not receive a certificate upon completion.

Further resources

Prospects is a well-known site for graduate jobs, internships, and graduate schemes:

www.prospects.ac.uk

The UK government also helps with career searching at:

www.gov.uk/find-a-job

Check out my book, for more essential tips and advice on how to make the most of your university experience, and in turn choose your perfect career:

Becker, L. (2019) *Study your way to your perfect career.* **London: Sage.**